hearing voices

poems by
barbara
ruth
saunders

En Route Books and Media, LLC
Saint Louis, MO

⊕ENROUTE
Make the time

En Route Books and Media, LLC
5705 Rhodes Avenue
St. Louis, MO 63109

Contact us at
contactus@enroutebooksandmedia.com

Cover Credit: Barbara Saunders
Copyright 2024 Barbara Saunders

ISBN-13: 979-8-88870-279-6

Acknowledgments

Daniel O'Connell, who transmitted
the poetry bug and helped edit this
collection

Hollie Hardy and the Saturday
Night Special Crew for the impetus
to write on a regular basis

Labor Fest Poets for feedback and
community

i

Credits

"One Drop" appeared in *Highland Park Poetry (online)* and *Tea Roots (online)*

"Wayfinding at Père Lachaise," appeared in *The Throwback Special* 2023

"Metamorphosis" appeared in *The Throwback Special* 2023

Table of Contents

Invocation

My father taught me how to slide
A vinyl album from its sleeve
Without touching the grooves
Drop it on the turntable's peg
Place the diamond stylus at the
    edge
Scratch the voices of the dead
Out of a spinning black disc
Right into the room

After Sap Comes Blood

Out we go to the yard, my
    grandmother and me
Not the garden with its roses, fig
    trees, and Sweet William
Not the field with cornstalks taller
    than my head
Through a thicket where creatures
    heard but not seen
Scamper at our feet
We walk for hours
She stops at a tree
Indistinguishable from its
    neighbors
Drives a spike through the bark
After sap comes blood
Red like mine
I always knew plants could bleed
No matter what the science books
    said
And that I was not crazy to be
    attached
To individual leaves
The way I love my favorite tooth

The View from the Tallest Building in the World

I took my grandfather's hand
Clicked my jaw to pop my ears
We rose and rose
To the crown of the Empire
Exited to the deck
Grandpa pitched his fedora back on
    his head
Put his hands at my waist
Hoisted me to the highest ring on
    the pedestal
Of the tower viewer
Coin slot fed, eyepieces in focus
The grid below crawled with
    crowds
Scrambling for footing
Like captive ants in a farm
He had made this climb every year,
    he said
Since he and the building were new
    to this place
Its construction, his prosperity,
Testaments to the rewards of hard
    work
And the possibility of progress
When I attempt to state my
    ambitions
In the time it took
To ride down from the 86th floor

I realize I never got back to the
ground
And so I suck at elevator speeches
And so I am a poet

A Visit to the Margaret Mitchell House

"Do you want to touch it?"
The wooden head of a lion
Guards the bedchamber
Where hard convalescence
Brought grievance and boredom
Together like ovum and sperm
And a rebel child came to life

Unimaginable author trifecta –
Pulitzer, movie deal, sales runner-
    up to the Bible
The apartment is the tour's last
    exhibit
After childhood journals
Where she turned the paper
    sideways
Wrote roughshod over the rule

Newspaper clips
Stories heisted from men's beats
Adversarial correspondence
With lawyers and publishers
And publishers' lawyers
She rubbed the lion's head for good
    luck
According to the cheery, cherubic
    docent

"Do you want to touch it?"
No one stepped forward, so I did
Stuck my hand right in the roaring
    mouth
Stroked the tongue
"Are you a writer, honey?"
 The woman asked
"The writers always touch it."

A Visit from the God of Time

A feral tomcat
Appeared on my block
He looks like a lynx
A gorgeous stud cheek
On his left side
On the right
Cancer eats out from the bone

Maybe, just maybe
Someone will catch him
Get him some treatment
Save his life
Lop off his jaw
Keep him caged for weeks
Radiate that tumor
Talk about solitary, poor, nasty,
    brutish, and short!

He looks straight at me
Reminds me of that famous statue
Of the two-faced Roman god of
    time
But so much uglier
And so much lovelier
In flesh and fur and blood and rot
Than in stone

Tooth and Claw

Black-and-white cat stomps
    through sunrise dream
Molars erupt from claw sheaths
Leave bite marks on my gray
    matter
Amid fragments of thought

Oh, impossible visitor!
Magical predator
Day stalker
Do you regret trading your
    precision slicers
For enamel grinders?
And what's in your mouth where
    teeth should be?
An empty stomach
A swollen uterus
A tell-tale heart dug up from the
    driveway

Alarm bells ring from the collar
    around your neck
Scatter the night birds
Rush hour song fills the air
Back you go to your hiding place
In the crawlspace under my breath

A Dream of Jerry Garcia

Jerry Garcia takes the stage at a
    nightclub
Despite the fact that he is dead.
The curtains part. There he sits on
    a stool.
White followspot and purple
    footlights stroke him
In ablutionary waves until
He folds closed along the spine like
    a hymnal
And vanishes.
Silence and relief fill the room
As the crowd files out.

Elvis' Eyes

I dreamed I lost Elvis' eyes
That's all I wrote on the pad
I keep near my bed
In hopes of capturing fleeting
    thoughts
Insight for living
Or material for some literary
    venture
But now I don't know
What those scrawled words even
    mean

How did I come to possess Elvis'
    eyes?
There might have been some
    legitimate
Chain of custody
It's my unconscious
I can do whatever I want
And so can the imagined Elvis
Maybe he gave me his eyes
As a reward for bringing him back
    to life
To allow him to sing and eat and
    pop pills again
Spar in the dojo again
All worth the toll of parting with
    his sense of sight

What was the condition of the
     eyes?
Documentation and memory both
     fail me
They might have been moist and
     warm
As if recently plucked
Cooled off and on their way to
     desiccation
Caked with crumbs from a reused
     Ziplock baggie
Or kept pristine in the Monday and
     Tuesday slots of a pillbox

How did I lose such treasures?
I might have carelessly tossed
     them,
Covered in lint,
When I emptied my pockets
Into the trash can at the
     laundromat
Maybe they will come out in the
     wash
As fleeting thoughts
Insight for living
Or material for some literary
     venture

Metamorphosis

I become a gull
Inch by inch, skin to plumage
Smile stiffens to keratin beak
Lashes fall like needles from dying
    evergreens
Eyes migrate out and shrink
Arms to wings, toenails to claws
Fish was never my favorite
With its aftertaste of newsprint
    and ink
Scooped just now from the tide
Victim wiggles in my mouth
Salty, springy flesh
Fish is wonderful
Lift off, meal moving still
Blood metallic
Like the shimmering silver scales
That gave her away as prey
Aloft, I ride earth's gusts
Trusting moments of suspension
    between exhalations
Gravity, a master who's lost my
    papers
This is free territory
As long as I can dodge
Power lines, hawks, owls
I was not so vigilant
Before I became a gull

One Drop

Icarus coveted the golden sun
But he was warned, too, to keep his
    distance from the sea
As the wax melted and the feathers
    drifted down
Icarus dove to break water's
    surface with wing tip
Twirled gleefully into a gyre
He didn't drown
The sea did what the sea will do
Cracked him apart
Pulverized marrow and burst every
    capillary
Dyed itself red like a sunset

2001: An Odyssey

If you live in the aftermath,
you're one of the lucky ones
Whatever scrap of you remains,
You have survived
Whether you want to be here or
    not.
You stand in line for hours to see a
    hole in the ground
Full of dust. The police officers
    guarding the site
Wear thicker gloves than you
    thought to bring
And bang their hands together
For warmth.

Manhattan's cold in February,
    though
And an ungodly chill rises from
    your bones
When your gaze catches the eyes
Rows and rows of them
In pairs, looking out from faces in
    photos on posters
Set between the word
"MISSING" in tall block letters
And fine print detailing when this
    person

Was last seen and who has been
    looking for them
Since September.

Blue, brown, hazel, green —
All gray ash now, in that pile that
    awaits
Around the corner or maybe
    floating
In this frigid air.
If you don't bear witness, what will
    you remember?
If you don't remember, who will?
If you live in the aftermath,
you're one of the lucky ones
Whatever scrap of you remains,
You have survived.
Whether you want to be here or
    not.

Cutaway

One day you're dancing the tango
To a private orchestra
On New Year's Eve
In a cutaway that makes your
shoulders
Look chiseled as the David
And invites a hand down the length
of your back
Oh, how they ogle
Mistake the shine from your shoes
For a light in
Your eyes
You glide across the slippery tile
Without a single misstep
Before you know it, the party has
ended
You toast with vodka again and again
(And again and again)
Raise a glass to that face in the
mirror
You hope is a ghost come to haunt
you
The alternative being so much worse
to contemplate
When the fringes of the carpet catch
your toes
There is no one there to stop the fall

A Fleeting Understanding

The pensioners complain
As they wait for the bus
To take them to Arlington National
    Cemetery
The hotel room was too cold at
    night and
Too hot in the morning
The summer sun, too bright

When offered a choice at the
    visitors' center
Between riding and marching
Along the path of tombstones
Every customer rejects the idea of
    a shuttle,
Then, huffing and puffing,
    complains again

They talk over the tour guide,
Who recounts the sorrows
Of captives who labored here under
    the lash
Of the traitor-general's kin, pushed
    out
By vengeful bureaucratic
    maneuver,
Their rose garden littered with
    corpses

And of all who earned those pretty
    plots
The hard way

Soldiers sweat in wool coats,
Guarding the unknowns,
Steady as the oaks nursing
    wounded roots
Cut with a chainsaw to make way
For fresh graves

Teenage tourists stop to read the
    inscription
That captions the eternal flame --
"The torch has been passed to a
    new generation."
-- And they manage, for a moment,
    to behave

Coq au Vin
and Clairefontaine

The waiters wear black bow ties
And crisp white shirts
Serve ice cream sundaes for
    breakfast
(Strawberry's the best)
And the cheapest dish on the menu
    is
Coq au vin et pommes frites
The Loire Valley equivalent
Of the burger and fries
Time capsule of the 1950s
A stroll away, over cobblestone
There's an ancient cathedral
Where between communion wafer
And ceremonial wine
One kisses the tombs of children
Buried there in the 1500s
A Clairefontaine French-ruled
    notebook
Holds a shopping list for tonight's
    dinner
And my hopes for the long future

Pandemic Summer

June 2020

Crows cruise the sidewalks
Cawing to each other about whether
Freedom to roam is worth it
With crumbs so scarce

Downy woodpeckers gorge themselves
Because bugs and bark
taste better
Without the smoky flavor of auto
    exhaust

Sparrows learn to pose
For primates who stare
From behind the glass
Hour after hour after hour

Dogs shiver and hide
As fireworks that won't be used in
    July
Go off night after night
As if there was reason to celebrate

The rats are hungry
and at war with one another
like shoppers in the toilet paper aisle
in March
The cats observe all the fuss

From sunspots and soft chairs,
From pillows cradling the heads of
    nappers,
From porches facing calm, quiet
    streets

Middle Age

One day you wake up in exile
The past over yonder moat of time

A thousand imagined futures
Exposed as mirage

Going – going – gone, the people
Who recognize your ancient tongue

Can dance the steps to the music you
    hum
Try as you might to rest in the Now,

The present is a foreign land

After 40 Years of Counting Down the Days to Retirement

The day after he collected the gold
    watch,
He freaked. He was sure the birds
    screeching at 5am
Mocked his lack of industriousness
And earthworms tugged at his
    ankles,
Like restaurant patrons poking
At lobsters in a tank.
When his wife served his favorite
    heart attack on a plate
She skipped her admonition that he
    control his portions.
That gesture of sympathy and
    indulgence
Aroused suspicion, not gratitude.
Then his Great Dane galloped over to
    his fear,
Uncertainty, and doubt and marked
    them with piss.
Buried that gold watch in the yard,
    where bones go for later.
Because the dog lives in eternity
Meat fills the belly
Apple trees drop dessert for the
    taking
The fetch ball remains in flight.

Surprise Sestina

Spring was my time
Adventure at full force
Every day a revealed
Secret. Life, so tender.
A womb-pink sky at equinox
A drop of fresh cream

What a surprise when the cream
Began to curdle, signaled passing
    time
That dark September equinox
Light taken by force
Like hard-earned legal tender
Snatched, extent of debt revealed

Months and years revealed
Heavy, sweet cream
Churned into a tender
Balm to heal the tongue, like the
    time
I drank warm milk after Grandma
    tried to force
Hot peppers on me one febrile
    equinox

That old wives' cure in equinox
Cusp of old to new medicines
    revealed
Breaking away, a tour-de-force

Ordeal of cold cream
Loving care for wrinkles of time
Cheeks and rebel lips still tender

What is left to tender
With the returning equinox
The sky this time
Red. Afire. A coming harvest.
    Wisdom revealed
Exchanging lemons at tea for
    cream
Predictable pleasure, claimed full
    force

Will to love life, its own force
No room to be tender
When the universe wants to cream
Me, moon after solstice after
    equinox
Only a subset of knowledge is ever
    revealed
A few markers of time

Cream-white clouds force
Time to hide the tender
Tipping this equinox; winter
    revealed

Remember

That when you almost lost it
The man who didn't love you
Nonetheless stroked your cheeks
Held your hand
Directed your thoughts
From the cacophony in your mind
To the melodic lifeline
Coming through the speakers

People should know how to do this
Those who can are remembered
For more than the dark curls
Time takes from them
Or the eyes that will shine
　　unchanged
From their elderly faces

To Those Who Would
Leave the Womb

It never happens
The memory of that particular
    blood
Colors your consciousness

The pulse of that drum
Beats with your own
In cross-rhythm
Or in lockstep like a John Phillip
    Sousa march
Breaks through every song you
    ever hear
With choruses of love and self-
    loathing
Breaks your heart if you try to tune
    it out
Those chords ring forever
Each after the next
A familiar chorale you don't
    memorize
Just recognize when you find it

Throw your dance card in the
    campfire
While it burns by starlight
A hundred perfect sparks
Rise and fade
And incarnation is enough

I Know Now

*After Lucille Clifton, for Ruth
    Westheimer*

When my mother told me
I came out face first
I imagined myself
Neck craned
Head held high
Glaring impatiently
At my spacious new home
Staring life down

I know now
That babies can't do that
Face first, sunny side up
Means I came into the world
On my back
Turned to the blazing sky
The birds, the stars, the beyond
Ready to love the heat and light

Strange Days

The day the sky turned orange as a caution cone, my iPhone took perfect pictures of the saffron-colored blossoms in my neighbor's yard. Explanations came fast to mollify the people, already panicked from the wildfires and zoonotic virus: Fog and smoke filtered the sun. Nothing to worry about here. A scientist named Marr described the ten plagues as an easily explained causal chain of events. A rabbi told the *New York Times*, "God often works in natural ways."

Cafe Ohlone,
During Lockdown

The tribes never left. Where would
    they go?
The elders made maps to the
    gathering grounds,
names of the plants and animals,
and all the ancient recipes in English
    and Spanish

They hid the translations from the
    children
Until they were sure the youngsters
    knew
The community's own language,
Loved it in their mouths
As much as they loved the perfume of
Grandma's sweat at the end of a
    workday,
Grandpa's breath when he kissed
    them.

On the patio behind a Berkeley
    bookstore
Foreigners like me paid by the plate
To learn in our guts
What it might be like to be from here
Here
To have a here to be from

Until globetrotters gobbling
    experiences and cash
Like the colonists before them
    swallowed up land
Tracked germs again across Ohlone
    territory
Now the tables of welcoming and
    forgiveness
Sit empty and quiet
The website reads,
"We have seen this before.
We know what to do."

Wayfinding
at Père Lachaise

Paris, 2023

I mingle with the resting dead
Silent in their sepulchers

Laid beneath sculptures that weep
    forever
Or gravestones covered in lipstick

A woman drags a hard-shell
    suitcase
and holds a paper map

She's as lost as I am
Looking for Jim Morrison

Carrion crows cackle
At our hilarious earthbound
    wandering

"C'est trop compliqué!"
Says the woman, of the maps

Charting jumbled neighborhoods
Where the deceased mock the
    borders of centuries

An elfin man startles us
Anticipates our plea

"Je vais vous accompagner," he
    says,
Promising to rescue our pilgrimage
    from purgatory

I struggle to translate
The stories he tells of this place

Like the one of a girl
who dies after tumbling into the
    tomb of her mother

My ankles, my knees, my toes
Ache from the walk on cobblestone

We find Jim Morrison's tomb
A family cracks open bottles of
    beer

They make a toast in Portuguese to
    the Lizard King
And snap selfies

He has a new headstone
Since my last visit

It reads "Truthful to his own
     spirit"
Finally, my sign

One must die
But tombs of the artists don't sit
     alone

Pop stars, painters, poets — our
     mourners have needs!
Actors, composers, musicians —
     the spotlight will remain on
     your remains!

Make people feel, and the royalties
     keep coming
in the eternal currency of fresh
     tears

Bio

Barbara grew up in Westchester
County, New York, lives in Berkeley,
CA, and occupies

https://linktr.ee/barbararuthsaunders

on the web.

www.ingramcontent.com/pod-product-compliance
Lightning Source LLC
Chambersburg PA
CBHW070751050426
42449CB00010B/2425